RED ROSES

Poetry by Selima Hill

BOOKS

Saying Hello at the Station (Chatto & Windus, 1984)*

My Darling Camel (Chatto & Windus, 1988)*

The Accumulation of Small Acts of Kindness (Chatto & Windus, 1989)

A Little Book of Meat (Bloodaxe Books, 1993)

Trembling Hearts in the Bodies of Dogs: New & Selected Poems
(Bloodaxe Books, 1994): includes work from titles asterisked above,
the complete text of *The Accumulation of Small Acts of Kindness*,
and a new collection, *Aeroplanes of the World*

Violet (Bloodaxe Books, 1997)

Bunny (Bloodaxe Books, 2001)

Portrait of My Lover as a Horse (Bloodaxe Books, 2002)

Lou-Lou (Bloodaxe Books, 2004)

Red Roses (Bloodaxe Books, 2006)

CASSETTE

The Poetry Quartets: 2 (The British Council/Bloodaxe Books, 1998)
[with Fleur Adcock, Carol Ann Duffy & U.A. Fanthorpe]

Selima Hill

Red Roses

BLOODAXE BOOKS

Copyright © Selima Hill 2006

ISBN: 1 85224 740 1

First published 2006 by
Bloodaxe Books Ltd,
Highgreen,
Tarset,
Northumberland NE48 1RP.

www.bloodaxebooks.com
For further information about Bloodaxe titles
please visit our website or write to
the above address for a catalogue.

Bloodaxe Books Ltd acknowledges
the financial assistance of
Arts Council England, North East.

ARTS COUNCIL
ENGLAND

Cover printing by J. Thomson Colour Printers Ltd, Glasgow.

Printed in Great Britain by
Bell & Bain Limited, Glasgow.

This book is dedicated to the men I love

ACKNOWLEDGEMENTS

My thanks are due to the Royal Literary Fund for my fellowship at the University of Exeter, and in particular to Andy Brown at the School of English and to Steve Cook, the Royal Literary Fund Fellowship Officer.

CONTENTS

Nobody Stops Us

Nobody stops us
climbing into the cars
and heading off
towards a place they know
that's piled high
with bedding they can chew,
they can and do,
they chew and gobble everything,
they pin us to the bedding, chewing everything,
and screwing up our faces under chests
that curl with hairs like flies who've got no heads
and have to be content with their genitals.

They Like to Keep Us Well Battened Down

They like to keep us well battened down!
And when they're done
how tired we all are!
Suddenly it's all about forgiveness.
Suddenly it's all about love.
Together we remember to remember:
never go to sleep without a hug.
Never go to sleep!
It's not worth it.
Remember they've been waiting all their lives.
Pinch yourself.
Be vigilant
like lizards.
Terrible things happen when you sleep.

The Fact Is That It's Everywhere

The fact is that it's everywhere like gas.
We learn how not to sleep
and not to scream
and how to rush outside for gulps of air –
we gulp it down in lungsfull like great rocks!
The worst thing we can do is go to sleep.
Think of it as like an orange plain
where slender horses vanish in the heat
and screams from falling riders can be heard
vibrating on the edge of pain and pleasure.
We learn how not to move and not to breathe.
We learn to nip the pleasure in its bud;
we learn to nip the pleasure in its bud
like savage mothers with enormous teeth.

This Is What It's Like

This is what it's like when we're born.
This is how the night follows day,
this is how they smoulder in hot cars
and steadfastly refuse
to be forgivable,
this is how they grip their leather steering-wheels,
spattering the verges with hot mud.
Mothers are advised to keep quiet.
Babies are advised to die now.
They say you'll be all right but you won't.
Slip away while Jesus says you can.
Life is for experiencing Love
and people do.
Other people don't.
Slip away to Jesus while you can.

Our Softness Is Appalling

Our softness is appalling and untouchable,
it whimpers like the gowns of married men
that perish in the darkness of tall wardrobes
that stretches from our bedrooms to Japan
where every thing that happens happens softly
and love is like a bag of warm eyeballs
passed from hand to hand in the dark.

Terrible Things Happen When We Hope

Terrible things happen when we hope
and terrible things happen when we smile:
every smile betrays a little hope
and terrible things happen when we hope.

They Tell Us We Know Nothing

They tell us we know nothing but we do.
We know their voice;
we know what it will say.
We know it's near
and that it's full of love
and that this love is in the form of pain.

They Tell Us We Know Nothing But We Do

They tell us we know nothing but we do.
We know about brutality:
it's sweet.
It's private
and obscene
like mother's milk.
A little bit goes a long way.
(My little bit has lasted fifty years!)
Every day we do what we can.
We bottle it
and keep it in our larders,
tucked away.
Our luminous preserve!

Down Between Our Little Thighs

Down between our little thighs their mouths
chomp and chew us like the mouths of dogs
that chew their rubber toys beneath white stars
that can't believe how savagely they chomp.

They Stuff Our Mouths with Sausages

They stuff our mouth with sausages like sandwiches
and anyone who wriggles will be tickled
and wrapped and rolled in body-parts like bandages
and anyone who makes it through the night
shudders like a little gold toboggan
that's been flying over tree-tops in a snowdrift
that stretches from the end to the beginning
of somewhere where there's no one there to find us
and no one there to hunt the padded hunters
that tear at us and tear at us like bears.

It's Dark Between Our Thighs

It's dark between our thighs.
It's like a garden
where everything and everyone gets lost
and all night long they crawl and grunt like babies
down avenues of bruises' yellow roses.

They're Sick and Tired of All This Hanging Around

They're sick and tired of all this hanging around!
They need to just get on with it and do it,
they need to just get in there, and push,
and push and push our heads between their knees
and grip us till we fall apart like jelly
that nurses kindly spoon into a heap
on sheets as unfamiliar as lay-bys.

Our Private Parts

Our private parts aren't private at all!
Strangers like to cuddle them and smell them
and poke at them
like animals in cages
whose bottoms are as bald as ripe plums.

Underneath Our Pretty Summer Dresses

Underneath our pretty summer dresses
grow gardens of blue bruises like blue roses –
none of which understand anything!
They spend their lives trying to be pink
and dreaming of a god in perfect trousers.

They Always Think They're Right

They always think they're right,
and we are wrong,
which makes them very angry all the time,
stamping and crashing about,
while we are quiet –
wrong, but quiet –
which we prefer.

Terrible Things Happen in the Summer

Terrible things happen in the summer.
Terrible things happen when it's hot.
Terrible things happen in hot zoos
where kangaroos scritch and scratch their tails.
Terrible things happen when the sick
run upstairs expecting to be cuddled
and rocked in tender laps
and when they're not.

When They Walk Towards Us

When they walk toward us
darkness falls,
desolations falls,
as on a chicken farm:
they walk towards us
to extract our hearts
and freeze them in stacked blocks
they can saw.

Our Job Is to Forget We Are Human

Our job is to forget we are human.
Our job is to be calm as a vest.
Our job is to arrange for the arrival
of angels, by the coachload, in white vests.
Our job is to be dim and indestructible.
Our job is to be white as newborn vests.

They Ram Themselves with Thumps Between Our Thighs

They ram themselves with thumps between our thighs
and pour with sweat, like tipped-up Golden Syrup tins;
they jam themselves inside our leaky thighs
like mattresses inside abandoned mini-bars
where, deep within the vales of blue snow,
loneliness has built her secret palaces
that glitter like the tears of billionaires
nobody will ever find their way to:
the corridors are long,
the stairs are icy,
the lifts controlled by grubby-looking angels
who spend their days alone on distant landings
crushing heads between the closing doors.

We Ourselves Experience It As Lumps

We ourselves experience it as lumps
no one wants to have to think about,
far less understand,
far less touch –
except of course the tall fragrant doctor
whose slicing skills are famous
and unstoppable,
who slices here and there with gay abandon,
his blazing theatres throbbing with white light:
see his dainty plastic-coated fingers
skimming purple lumps into buckets
that overflow goodnaturedly on boots
as chunky as the paws of polar bears
that kill a person – bam! – just like that,
that kill to kill,
that kill and never stop,
that scrape and scoop until their paws are raw
and everything's gone red
like blood-red roses.

See the Flies

See the flies, delirious with joy,
on summer afternoons in tiled rooms
where roses part like thighs on polished sideboards
in houses we refuse to call our home;
see the flies, delirious with joy,
plunging blindly into fresh wounds.

Like Diners Pouring Syrup

Like diners pouring syrup through dark hallways
and treading it about on polished shoes
and spreading it about on caps and taps
and tiny moonlit sleepers like sardines,
like diners stumbling home
late at night,
they slap and stamp their swollen hands and feet –
listen.
Steady!
Hate will get us nowhere!
Hate will get us nowhere.
Don't we know that?
The diners' hands are handling us like gloves
full to bursting with reluctant syrup.

Love Is Like a Terrifying Angel

Love is like a terrifying angel.
We hate to hear its terrifying wings.
We hate to feel it crawling down our ears
like slugs in evening dresses down dark corridors
from which the sound of counting can be heard.

We Don't Know What It Is

We don't know what it is but this is it.
What we have to do is count to ten.
Count a little huddle of ten sheep.
Kneel by their sides.
It's OK.
Night will fall, bringing moths and sleep
and one by one the sheep will form a line
and tap their forty diamond-studded feet.
They'll tap and tap and tap and tap and tap.
Screaming cannot stop them nor can teeth.

We Learn to Stay at Home

We learn to stay at home
and stay well back
and creep along the corridors
like walls
and as we creep
we say what Fear says:
it says *placate*.
It says *placate placate*.

We Like to Do Our Best But We Can't

We like to do our best
but we can't.
We do our best to please them
but we don't.
We make mistakes again and again.
Why? Because we're stupid! We're so stupid
we feel homesick in our own homes!
We're homesick, and it hurts, but we're so stupid
we don't know what it is we're homesick *for*!
We snip and chop and swab and do our best
and all the time we feel sick at heart.
We shrink like shrimp inside our pretty dresses.
We shrink and rage inside our sticky hair.

We're Here to Look Our Best

We're here to look our best *and we do*.
We look our best even though it hurts.
It hurts so much it makes our hair fall out!
We shake with rage,
we grip the bars of buggies
and grip the tiny shoulders of thin children
we button up ferociously in coats.
Motherhood itself is like a coat!
Mothers have to wear them all the time,
even here, along this burning bench
that echoes with interminable sobbing.

We Learn to Marvel at the Golden Hair

We learn to marvel at the golden hair.
We learn to marvel at the knee-length arms
that like to feel their way to upstairs bedrooms
as white and soft as bedrooms made of flour.

Day and Night Don't Matter Any More

Day and night don't matter any more
and all that matters now is being cold.
Too bad we're cold.
Too bad it isn't easy.
Too bad our skin is turning blue with cold.
Isn't blue the colour of devotion?
And doesn't it get easier and easier?
Being this aware is kind of bliss!
Don't they know that?
Don't they know that vigilance
is always watching over us like hawks?

They Crash About Our Living-rooms

They crash about our living-rooms like aeroplanes
crushing trees and crashing into rocks
and strewing flowery mountainsides with passengers
whose sons will not be coming to collect them.

When We're Bored

When we're bored and lonely we go shopping!
We cross the pavement with our little bags
and make our way in haste to the station.
I wonder what will catch our eyes this time!
Perhaps a hat!
Perhaps a pair of shoes!
We're aiming for a bit of distraction!
We're aiming to forget the stubby fingers
riffling through our hairdos like the Pope
(even though he *is* the Pope) might ruffle
Our Lady's veil, to reach Our Lady's lips,
from which a stream of sunlight can be seen
lighting up a mattress where a man,
accompanied by several scowling women
whose skin is red
like roses in a rose-bowl,
enjoys his favourite way of being naked –
several of his favourite ways, in fact.

Look, a Golden Knee

Look, a golden knee can just be seen
being gripped and twisted by large hands
that work too hard to notice we are beautiful,
so beautiful that if we're touched we sing!

Overwork Is Just a Kind of Laziness

Overwork is just a kind of laziness
for people who enjoy being thin.
It twinkles on the foreheads of the meek
and by the afternoon a warm cascade
rumbles down their necks
like scarlet rocks.
Workers roll on workers with such diligence
everyone forgets how to stop!
They keep themselves alive by drinking coffee
and then by thinking thoughts of being dead
but when they find they really are dying
then they hear it call across the city,
across the golden halls –
that place called Home!
It's easy to be lazy when you're dead
but first they want to laze around at home!

We Think We Think They Love Us

We think we think they love us
but we don't.
We creep about unloveably
like insects
creeping about with half their legs torn off.

Like Glaciers Weighed Down By Being Cold

Like glaciers
weighed down by being cold
grinding frozen lakes
on lonely nights,
they grind us down,
they grind us without mercy:
our private parts respond like frozen shrimp
who can't respond
because they've got no sea.

We Sometimes Think They're Listening

We sometimes think they're listening
but they're not –
how *could* they be
when they've got no ears?
Their heads are blunt.
Blunt and thick like gloves.
Their brains are like the world's smallest wall.
Their hearts are like a wall made of icicles
dipped in concrete
so they never move:
concrete puts a stop to all movement
and with its creamy blankets brings peace.

Whack Us on the Head

Whack us on the head!
And again!
And watch the blood bubble in our hair
and watch our skin turn from pink to blue
and watch us going limp.
And again!
Don't they know our heads are hanging off?
No they don't.
They haven't a clue.

They Lie in Wait

They lie in wait for lips on which to binge –
and binge they do,
they binge until they drop,
they binge and bulge like little bloated puppies
that roll around the bedroom like their sins
(though only Jesus washes *those* away!)

They Told Us They Were Strong

They told us they were strong
and we believed them;
they told us they were kind,
but they weren't.
They told us that they loved us
but, my friend,
if they really loved us we would know!
Some of us fooled ourselves, briefly,
then fell apart,
like the perfect rose.

How Dangerous and Beautiful It Is

How dangerous and beautiful it is
to kneel in the dust at their feet.
Don't worry if we don't understand!
No one does!
This is what it's like!
This is what it's like to feel happy.
This is where they come in nice and close.
And this is where they like to make suggestions.
And this is where we slither to our knees.
What's the point of being upright anyhow?
It's safer to be stacked in special bays,
with blindfolds on, and rope between our legs.

Hush

Hush, there's someone coming,
grab a towel
and brush the lips and hair of sullen daughters
whose perfect man is actually a horse
on which to gallop to their heart's content
perched above the thundering flanks and buttocks.

We Are at the Mercy of Their Mercy

We are at the mercy of their mercy
and if you contradict us you are wrong.
We don't know what they do
but they do it.
They do it till they drown in it like bulls.

We May Not Have Their Valour and Their Beards

We may not have their valour and their beards
but what we've got instead is our shoes:
we step into our shoes as into chambers
lined with tongues that love to lick warm toe-nails!

If We Stop, Even for One Second

If we stop, even for one second,
diners will appear,
demanding roasts,
and light –
what light there is –
will start to fail
and now, my friends,
we need to slip away,
slip away and sit completely still
like someone with a zebra in her lap
who folds his brittle legs like polished handkerchiefs
and sleeps for ever,
dreaming of warm milk.

They Stride Across the Tarmac

They stride across the tarmac to brown aeroplanes
that have no room today or any day
for any woman with imperfect teeth,
imperfect ears or imperfect handbags,
whose families will discover them years later
rocking in the passages of hospitals.

We Want to Love Each Other

We want to love each other
but we can't.
We want to but it's hard
so we don't.
All we do is glare at the sky
whose yellow stars twinkle up above.
We glare at them until we can't go on.
We ask them to have mercy.
But they won't.
They blink their yellow blinks and sail on.

Everything

Everything and everybody glitters.
They glitter too,
like snails stuck with sand.
Every grain of dust and sand must glitter.
And, tucked up tight between our thighs, our hairs,
like filed rings, itch and glitter too.

Our Brains Are Like the Brains of Dried Peas

Our brains are like the brains of dried peas
that have no brains
and cannot disobey
and cannot understand how not to swell
as lips like juices make us into soup.

No one Comes

No one comes.
No one takes our hand.
Our dresses twitch
like dresses full of finches:
anyone approaching
must take care.

They Walk as if They're Stepping Over Bodies

They walk as if they're stepping over bodies;
they walk as if they're hated,
which they are;
they walk around like birds the size of overcoats
with hands like claws that pin us to the ground.

We're Living in a Place Where Prayer Begins

We're living in the place where prayer begins
but are our prayers beginning? No, they're not,
they're frozen on our lips like frozen whortleberries
stuck together in white frozen lumps.

We Stroke Our Necks

We stroke our necks,
we stroke each other's necks,
we stroke and scratch the necks and ears of horses
and go to sleep with tears in our eyes
and pillows in our mouths like lumps of concrete:
we can't believe that this is who we are!
We can't believe that this is how we live,
that every night is like a long journey
sharing nothing with a severed head.

They Like to Fill Us Up

They like to fill us up at top speed!
They like to fill us up to the brim!
They fill us up so full we tip and leak.
Our pubic hairs keep sticking to the sheet.
They fill us up and wish we'd go to hell
where we can be as sticky as we like.

Finally They Grunt

Finally they grunt
and roll over
and silence settles over us
like sorrow.

They Go to Work

They go to work, they work, they go back home
but something isn't right.
They don't know what.
As heavy plums gather in hot gardens
they gather in hot bars with laughing strangers
whose little necks they get to squeeze and fondle.

Be Like Us

Be like us!
Never smile.
Sob.
Sob for drips, a fuck, a cigarette,
Sob for Heaven like the sobbing sick,
Sob for nurses, sob for medication.
Could it be they love us?
I don't think so!
Give it up.
Give up everything.
To smile is to say *I am sick.*

This Is Not the Time to Start

This is not the time to start talking!
This is not the time to say we're suffering.
They haven't got all day, you know. *Quick quick!*
Shut your mouth or get the hell out.

They Take One Look

They take one look and have to look away!
O, wouldn't it be wise if they could take us
and pop us in a little drawer like lingerie,
smelling not of blood but summer meadows
where coloured flowers flower as expected
and coloured beetles live without love.
Love is like a large warm knife.
We keep it in a bag in our handbags.

Our Dream

Our dream is to design the perfect dress
whose icy sheath will grip us like a vice
and hold us steady till we freeze to death
and every little pore will be at rest
and golden hairs will rest from being warm.

When We Put Their Dinner Down

When we put their dinner down
they growl.
First they growl and then they start to bite.
They bite and chew anything in sight.
We do our best to keep their dishes full,
we fill them up again and again,
and even when they fall asleep at last
we rush and put their dinner down *again*!

They Must Of Course Be Fed Completely Separately

They must of course be fed completely separately
with separate knives and forks
at separate tables
that cannibals have carried day and night
up and down the tracks of rocky valleys
that yield neither virgins nor football.

First We Make Them Comfy

First we make them comfy on the sofa
and then we sit and watch them fall asleep ...
their coffee's getting cold on the coffee-table ...
O when they've got their shoes off they're so cute!

They Twiddle Us

They twiddle us as if we were machines.
They twiddle with our nipples and our noses.
They twiddle –
and when everyone's gone home
they fall on us and tear us apart!
It's not about forgiveness any more.
How can we forgive them when they're blameless?
They don't know what they're doing.
And they're cute.
Yes, we have to pacify them first –
by 'pacify' we mean remove the shoes
weighing down their feet like giant chops!
Once pacified and upsidedown, they're cute!

Every Night We Do Our Best To Love Them

Every night we do our best to love them
and some of us actually *do* love them!
They stay at home together in warm pairs
and snuggle up and watch the hours go by
like trays of strawberry jam and strawberry jelly.
And those who don't
look up to those who do
and marvel at them
as one might at fur
that seems to know exactly what it's doing.

Searching Searching

Searching, searching,
on our stiff red legs,
here we come,
searching yet again,
searching through the bedrooms and the boardrooms
for somebody to *run to*
and *cling to*;
searching till we drop
like amputees
who only want the night to bring them satin.

Every Night Imaginary Cows

Every night imaginary cows
come and stand beside us in our room
and gaze at us with disappointed eyes.
These are the cows of shame.
They will not budge.

Nobody Sees Them

Nobody sees them,
nobody hears the cars,
nobody finds the little place they know
where diners go to barbecue their cats;
nobody knows, nobody cares
how scared they are
of anything big and beautiful like night.

Just Because It Looks Too Dark

Just because it looks too dark to them
doesn't mean it looks too dark to us
and doesn't mean to say we won't go in.
If nothing else, they need to know we will.
They need to know we need to go right in
where beams of sun- and moonlight never seep
and nothing moves except the lack of light
becoming aware of a place where nothing falters
and nothing happens that we can't forgive.

They Come to Us To Swim

They come to us to swim
but they drown.
They come to us like horses to a lake
that glitters in the dazzling sun
like scissors,
they come to us and drown
like wild horses
drowning in the lakes of private palaces
with birds and fish entangled in their hair.

Leave Them

Leave them.
They must never be disturbed.
Our mothers hated everything about us
and so do they.
Never smile at them.